The Must-Have Chinese Cookbook for You

Chinese Cooking Made Simple for Everyone

BY: Allie Allen

COOK & ENJOY

Copyright 2019 Allie Allen

Copyright Notes

This book is written as an informational tool. While the author has taken every precaution to ensure the accuracy of the information provided therein, the reader is warned that they assume all risk when following the content. The author will not be held responsible for any damages that may occur as a result of the readers' actions.

The author does not give permission to reproduce this book in any form, including but not limited to: print, social media posts, electronic copies or photocopies, unless permission is expressly given in writing.

Table of Contents

Delicious Chinese Food Recipes.................................. 7

Chapter I - Appetizers... 8

1) Chinese Mushrooms... 9

2) Chinese Chicken Wings 10

3) Turkey Potstickers 12

4) Oriental Beans and Peppers 14

5) Chestnut Kabobs.. 15

6) 5 Spice Boy Choy 17

7) Thyme Eggs 18

8) Sweet Bok Choy 20

9) Chinese Pizza Pancakes................................. 21

10) Sesame Tofu.. 23

Chapter II - Stir fry.. 24

11) Citrus Shrimp Stir Fry 25

12) Beef Fry 27

13) Grilled Chicken Teriyaki Stir Fry 29

14) Shrimp Stir Fry 31

15) Gaelic Stir Fry 33

16) Honey Ginger Pork Stir Fry 35

17) Greek Stir Fry 37

18) Turkey Stir Fry 39

19) Tofu Veggie Stir Fry 41

20) Seafood Stir Fry 43

Chapter III - Soups 46

21) Chinese Chicken Soup 47

22) Peppered beef and lo mein noodle soup 49

23) Coconut Rice Soup 51

24) Not-so-traditional Wonton Soup 53

25) Hot and Sour Soup 55

26) 5 Ingredient Egg Drop Soup 58

27) Broccoli Soup 59

28) Tofu Ma Po 61

29) West Lake Steak 63

30) Corn Soup 65

Chapter IV - Main Dishes 66

31) Orange Chicken 67

32) General Tso Chicken 69

33) Shiitake Lo Mein 72

34) Tempura Chicken Lo Mein 74

35) Baby Back Ribs in Kicked Up Hoisin Sauce 76

36) Sweet and Sour Pork 79

37) Quick and Tasty Egg Rolls 80

38) Kung Pao Shrimp 83

39) Shiitake Lo Mein 85

40) Beef and Bok Choy 87

41) Shrimp Lo Mein 89

42) Fried Rice.. 91

43) Spiced Tofu.. 93

Chapter V - Sauces 95

44) Honey Teriyaki for Grilling 96

45) Easy Homemade Sweet and Sour 97

46) Take 5 Peanut Sauce 99

47) 1 Hour BBQ Sauce... 100

48) 300 Second Sauce 101

49) Ginger Thyme Oil... 102

50) Kicked Up Hoisin Sauce.. 104

51) Oriental Vinaigrette... 105

52) Tangy Teriyaki Sauce.. 106

53) T.A.G Sauce 107

About the Author.. 108

Author's Afterthoughts... 110

Delicious Chinese Food Recipes

SSSSSSSSSSSSSSSSSSSSSSSSSSSSSSSSSSSSSSSSSSSSSSSSSS

Chapter I - Appetizers

SSSSSSSSSSSSSSSSSSSSSSSSSSSSSSSSSSSSSSSSSSSSSSSSSSSS

1) Chinese Mushrooms

Tip- to ground cashews put in a plastic baggie, make sure it's sealed well, and roll over repeatedly with rolling pin;

Serving Sizes: 4-6

List of Ingredients:

- 13 large shitake mushrooms; organic, cleaned, and stems removed
- ½ pound ground chicken or turkey
- 1 stalk scallion, finely diced, divided
- ½ cup cashews, ground and divided
- Dash 5 spice

ssssssssssssssssssssssssssssssssssssssssssssssssssss

Procedure:

In wok or skillet cook chicken or pork according to package directions/temperatures; add half of cashews and dash of 5 spice. Mix well and let cook 1 minute. Remove from heat and let sit 3-5 minutes. 1 spoon full at a time top mushroom with chicken/pork mix, sprinkle the remaining scallions and cashews on top.

2) Chinese Chicken Wings

Serving Sizes: 4-6

List of Ingredients:

- 1 pound of chicken wings
- 1 cup honey
- 1 cup brown sugar
- 1/3 cup low sodium soy sauce
- 1 tbsp. red pepper flakes or paprika
- 1 tbsp. pineapple juice

sssssssssssssssssssssssssssssssssssssssssssssssssssssss

Procedure:

Preheat oven to 350 and prepare baking dish. In a small sauce mix together honey, brown sugar, soy sauce, red pepper flakes, and pineapple juice; stir until sugar dissolves and honey thins. Place wings in baking dish and with small basting brush "paint" sauce onto wings. Cover and store leftover sauce in refrigerator. Cook wings, covered for 45 minutes; remove covering re-apply sauce and cook 15 minutes. Insure chicken is done by cutting into one wing, if meat is still pink or running bloody juices cook for another 5-10 minutes. Warning, eating raw or undercooked chicken poses a health risk make sure it is fully done before serving and consuming.

3) Turkey Potstickers

This makes a lot of turkey mixture, if you have more than you need, you can freeze uncooked potstickers;

Serving Sizes: 40-45 potstickers

List of Ingredients:

- 1 pound ground turkey
- 1 tsp. butter
- 1 tsp. sesame oil
- 1 piece of ginger minced
- 1 stalk bok choy finely diced
- 2-3 scallions finely diced
- 1 tsp. celery salt
- 1 tsp. sriracha sauce
- 1 package potstickers
- Vegetable oil

sssssssssssssssssssssssssssssssssssssssssssssssssssss

Procedure:

In a deep pot or Dutch oven sauté butter, sesame oil, ginger, bok choy, and scallions; add turkey, celery salt, and sriracha sauce stir well and brown turkey. Lay out flat potstickers wrappers and fill 1 tsp., fold according to diagram. Brown both sides using thin layer of vegetable oil 1-2 minutes then add water and cover cook for 6-8 minutes. Let water totally evaporate potstickers will cook in the remaining oil; let this go on 2-3 more minutes.

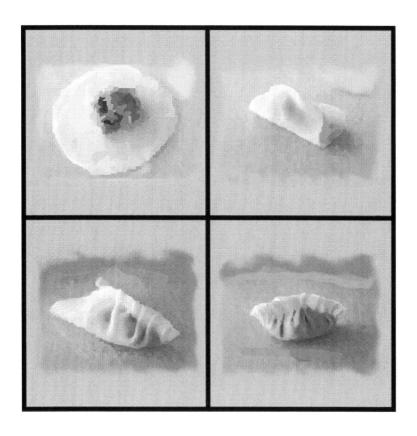

4) Oriental Beans and Peppers

Try this appetizer with different sauces and enjoy all the flavors this recipe has to give!

Serving Sizes: 4-6

List of Ingredients:

- 2 can (14.75) low sodium green beans, drained and washed
- 2 organic bell peppers, multiple colors if possible, washed and seeded
- 1 recipe 300 Second Sauce

ssssssssssssssssssssssssssssssssssssssssssssssssssss

Procedure:

In a bowl place beans and sauce and toss. Cut bell peppers into strips and put into bowl along with the beans. Toss; serve as is, or warm over med.-low heat.

5) Chestnut Kabobs

A favorite for Chinese New Year parties;

Serving Sizes: 5-7 kabobs.

List of Ingredients:

- 1 can diced chestnuts, drained and washed
- 1/3 cup honey
- 2 tbsp. pineapple juice
- ½ tbsp. brown sugar
- 2 tsp. ginger
- 1 tsp. turmeric
- 1 package turkey bacon

sssssssssssssssssssssssssssssssssssssssssssssssssss

Procedure:

Prepare a baking sheet and turn broiler on. In a saucepan mix together honey, pineapple juice, brown sugar, ginger, and turmeric. Keep over low heat and stir frequently until sugar dissolves and honey thins out. Remove from heat and let cool 2-3 minutes then pour into bowl followed by the water chestnuts. Coat well, wrap each individual piece with bacon, and stick on toothpick. Cook appetizer kabobs on skillet or grill 7-10 minutes.

6) 5 Spice Boy Choy

Usually this recipe is reserved for the adults; a kid friendly version is below.

Serving Sizes: 4

List of Ingredients:

- 4 stalks of organic bok choy, washed and diced
- 1 tbsp. low sodium soy sauce
- 1 /3- ¼ tsp. 5 spice powder

sssssssssssssssssssssssssssssssssssssssssssssssssssss

Procedure:

Prepare boy choy and place into small pot over med.-high heat. Add in soy sauce, 5 spice, and stir, let cook 1-2 minutes.

7) Thyme Eggs

A great protein snack,

Serving Sizes: 4

List of Ingredients:

- 4 eggs
- 4 cups of water, enough to ensure water level in pot is over eggs
- 1 ½ tbsp. soy sauce
- 3-5 fresh thyme leaves
- 3 tea bags

sssssssssssssssssssssssssssssssssssssssssssssssssss

Procedure:

Hard boil the eggs*. Remove the eggs, run under cold water and gently tap with the back of spoon to create a mosaic of jagged lines across the entire shell (be careful not to hit it so hard that the shell dislodges) Bring to boil and add soy sauce, thyme, tea leaves and eggs. Turn of burner and let sit 3-6 hours.

To hard boil an egg; bring water to a full boil. Insert eggs, remove from heat and let sit 18-22 minutes.

8) Sweet Bok Choy

Serving Sizes: 4

List of Ingredients:

- 4 stalks bok choy, washed and diced
- ¾ cup organic honey
- 3 tbsp. low sodium soy sauce

ssssssssssssssssssssssssssssssssssssssssssssssssssssss

Procedure:

Prepare boy choy and place into small pot over med.-high heat. Add honey, soy sauce, and stir, let cook 1-2 minutes.

9) Chinese Pizza Pancakes

Enjoy this version of a popular Chinese breakfast;

Serving Sizes: 4

List of Ingredients:

- 1 ¾ cup all-purpose flour
- 1 tsp. baking soda
- ¼ tsp. baking powder
- Dash salt
- 1 cup water
- 1 egg white
- 1 tsp. turmeric
- 1 cup diced scallions and bok choy
- Vegetable oil

ssssssssssssssssssssssssssssssssssssssssssssssssssssss

Procedure:

Mix flour, baking soda, baking powder, and salt, together in bowl. Add water, egg white, turmeric, and scallions/ bok choy. While mixing let burner be heating to high heat; mix should be liquid enough to be able to pour onto griddle; if not, add more water 1 tsp. at a time. Before cooking turn down burner to medium and pour mixture onto greased griddle. Cook 4-5 minutes on one side 3-4 minutes on the other.

10) Sesame Tofu

To mix it up try adding soy sauce to the pan and instead of pepper try 5 spice!

Serving Sizes: 5-8

List of Ingredients:

- 1 block firm tofu cut into 2x1 squares
- 2 tbsp. sesame oil
- Black pepper or red peppers flakes

sssssssssssssssssssssssssssssssssssssssssssssssssssss

Procedure:

Cut tofu and place it along with sesame oil in a hot skillet, do not crowd the tofu, you most likely will have to cook it in batches. Cook 7-8 minutes without disturbing but watching for a 'crust' to develop; when it does, flip them and cook 5 more minutes.

Chapter II - Stir fry

sssssssssssssssssssssssssssssssssssssssssssssssssss

11) Citrus Shrimp Stir Fry

Calamari, mussels, and clams make good substitutions or additions;

Serving Sizes: 4

List of Ingredients:

Meat

- 1-pound medium-large shrimp, cleaned, deveined, and tailed
- 1 tsp sesame oil
- 1 tbsp. pineapple juice
- ½ tbsp. organic honey
- ½ tbsp. brown sugar
- 1 tsp. cracked peppercorn
- 1 tsp. ginger powder or minced
- 1 tsp. low sodium soy sauce
- 1 tsp. orange peel

<u>Rice and Veggies</u>

- Cooked jasmine rice
- I cup chopped pineapple
- 2 chopped red and green pepper

ssssssssssssssssssssssssssssssssssssssssssssssssssss

Procedure:

In a plastic bag or air tight container put all of the Meat ingredients in refrigerator and marinade for 15-20 minutes. In wok or skillet empty all of the contents of the bag and cook until shrimp are no longer pink. Mix rice into shrimp mixture and stir.

12) Beef Fry

Serving Sizes: 3-4

List of Ingredients:

<u>Rice</u>

- 3 cups jasmine or basmati rice
- Enough beef broth to cook rice in
- 1 tbsp. sugar
- 1 tbsp. low sodium soy sauce
- Dash red pepper flakes

<u>Meat & Marinade</u>

- Shoulder steak or eye of round cut into thin strips or diced
- 1 recipe 1 Hour BBQ Sauce (see sauces for the recipe)

<u>Vegetables</u>

- 4 cherry tomatoes cut in half
- 1 head of broccoli
- 1/3 cup baby corn, drained

ssssssssssssssssssssssssssssssssssssssssssssssssss

Procedure:

Cook rice. Marinade steak and cook 1-2 minutes depending on how done you like your meat and mix in vegetables and rice. Mix together.

13) Grilled Chicken Teriyaki Stir Fry

A new flavor for a time honored dish;

Serving Sizes: 4

List of Ingredients:

<u>Meats and Veggies</u>

- 2, boneless and skinless chicken breasts or thighs diced
- ½ can bean sprouts
- 1 small can water chestnuts (diced)
- ½ block of tofu diced or crumbled
- ½ can, drained, baby corn
- 2 stalks diced bok choy
- 1 cup chopped Chinese cabbage
- 1 recipe honey teriyaki BBQ Sauce (see sauces), divided

Rice

- Cooked jasmine or brown rice

sssssssssssssssssssssssssssssssssssssssssssssssssssss

Procedure:

Marinate diced chicken for 2-4 hours in half of the teriyaki mix. When ready empty chicken, but not the marinade, into heated wok or skillet and cook 4-6 minutes. Add the remaining vegetables and teriyaki sauce; mix together and cook an additional 3-5 minutes. Serve over rice.

14) Shrimp Stir Fry

Serving Sizes: 4, also makes a great chilled dish just substitute lo mein for the rice.

List of Ingredients:

Marinade

- 2 tbsp. vegetable oil
- 1 tsp. pineapple juice
- 1-pound med. to large shrimp
- 1 tsp. onion powder
- 1 tsp. garlic powder
- 1 tsp. chili powder
- ½ piece of ginger minced of finely diced
- 1 tsp. sesame oil (optional)

<u>Rice</u>

- Cooked jasmine or brown rice
- Red and green bell peppers cut into strips
- 1 grated carrot
- 1-2 cups snow peas
- 1 small can crushed pineapple and remaining juice
- Sesame seeds (optional)

ssssssssssssssssssssssssssssssssssssssssssssssssssss

Procedure:

Fix ingredients for marinade, along with the shrimp, in a plastic bag or air tight container and let sit in the refrigerator 15-20 minutes. Once ready, empty contents of the bag into a wok or pot over medium-high heat and cook approx. 1-3 minutes (longer if large shrimp). Add to shrimp the rice, peppers, carrot, and peas; stir well and let ingredients warm through.

15) Gaelic Stir Fry

Serving Sizes: 4

List of Ingredients:

<u>Meats and Veggies</u>

- ½ cup vegetable oil or almond oil
- 1 pound beef cut into chunks or strips
- 1 can strained low sodium diced potatoes, if not low sodium wash thoroughly for 1-2 minutes
- 3 large carrots, washed and peeled, cut into 3-4 inch chunks
- ½ head of cabbage washed
- ½ cup baby corn
- 1/3 cup bean sprouts
- 1 recipe of 1 Hour BBQ Sauce (see sauces)

<u>Rice</u>

- Cooked white rice

sssssssssssssssssssssssssssssssssssssssssssssssss

Procedure:

Marinade meat and vegetables for 1 hour in plastic bag or air tight container in refrigerator. Empty contents of bag into heated wok or skillet and cook 5-7 minutes. Serve over warm rice.

16) Honey Ginger Pork Stir Fry

A tasty meal in little time!

Serving Sizes: 3

List of Ingredients:

<u>Meat</u>

- 1 cup shredded pork
- 1 tbsp. brown sugar
- 1 tbsp. organic honey
- ½ tbsp. low sodium soy sauce
- ½ tsp. garlic powder
- ½ tsp. ginger

<u>Rice-Veggies</u>

- 2 cups cooked jasmine or basmati rice
- 3 diced leek or 3 bok choy
- 1 yellow bell pepper
- 1 can bean sprouts or bamboo shoots
- 1 /4 cup organic, sliced & washed shitake mushrooms

SSS

Procedure:

In bowl mix together all of the ingredients listed under meats and set aside. Warm on a griddle or skillet over medium heat Turn of burner and serve over rice and veggies.

17) Greek Stir Fry

Culinary fusion at its best! For a delightful change, try the Ginger Thyme Oil

Serving Sizes: 4

List of Ingredients:

<u>Protein and Veggies</u>

- 2 cup shredded pork
- 1/3 cups black olives, pitted and sliced
- ½ tub roma or cherry tomatoes
- 1 red onion
- ½ cup spinach
- Greek oregano
- Mint leaves
- 1 recipe oriental vinaigrette
- Feta cheese, crumbled

<u>Rice</u>

- Cooked white or brown rice

sssssssssssssssssssssssssssssssssssssssssssssssssssss

Procedure:

Prepare all ingredients; over high heat in a wok or skillet heat all ingredients, except the sauce (oriental Vinaigrette) and the Feta cheese. Warm ingredients and place on top of warm rice. Top each plate with vinaigrette and Feta.

18) Turkey Stir Fry

A creative way to incorporate a cheap lean protein into your weekly menu!

Serving Sizes: 4

List of Ingredients:

<u>Marinade</u>

- 2 turkey tenderloins cut into cubes roughly 1 x 1
- 1-2 cups cubed tofu roughly 1 x 1
- 1 tbsp. low sodium soy sauce
- 1 tbsp. brown sugar
- ½ tsp. orange juice or pineapple juice
- 1/3 tsp. red pepper flakes

Rice and Veggies

- White or jasmine rice, cooked
- 1 stalk bok choy diced
- ½ cup cashews or macadamia nuts
- ½ cup grated carrot
- 1 cup broccoli trees
- ½ ginger grated (optional)

sssssssssssssssssssssssssssssssssssssssssssssssssssssss

Procedure:

Place all marinade ingredients into plastic bag or air tight container, mix well and refrigerate 35-40 minutes. Empty all marinade contents into heated wok or skillet; when done mix the rice and veggies into meat mixture and stir well. Once all is warm serve

19) Tofu Veggie Stir Fry

Great for vegetarians! Try it with different sauces and find out your favorite!

Serving Sizes: 4

List of Ingredients:

<u>Tofu and Veggies</u>

- 1 block of tofu cubes cut into 2x2
- 1 eggplant cut into 2x2 cubes
- Sautéed green beans or asparagus spears halved
- 2 cucumbers sliced into coin shaped rounds
- 2 large red of purple bell peppers (for the hotter palettes use habanero or jalapeno
- ½ cup kale
- 1/3 cup vegetable oil
- 1 recipe of T.A.G. sauce (see sauces section)

<u>Rice</u>

- Cooked jasmine or brown rice
- Black pepper (optional)

SSS

Procedure:

Prepare vegetables and put into a hot wok or skillet along with the sauce, cook 2-3 minutes. Serve over warm rice and top with pepper if desired.

20) Seafood Stir Fry

Get a dose of omega 3! Works well with various types of seafood and fish;

Serving Sizes: 4

List of Ingredients:

<u>Protein</u>

- ½ pound large to medium shrimp with the tails removed
- ½ pounds scallops
- ½ pound calamari
- 2 fillets cod, cubed
- 1 tsp. oyster sauce
- 1 tsp. chili powder
- 1 cup white wine
- 1/3 cup low sodium soy sauce

Rice and Veggies

- Cooked jasmine or brown rice or lo mein noodles
- 1 red pepper, washed and seeded sliced into strips
- Peppercorns or white salt
- Scallions, diced for garnish
- 1 tbsp. butter
- 1 tsp. brown sugar
- 1 tbsp. honey
- 1 tsp. pineapple juice or water
- 1 sweet onion cut in strips

sssssssssssssssssssssssssssssssssssssssssssssssssss

Procedure:

Prepare proteins and in a plastic bag or airtight container marinade seafood in oyster sauce, chili powder, white wine, and soy sauce for 15 minutes. Heat a wok or skillet to high and turn down to medium just before placing butter, brown sugar, honey, juice or water and let mix together until smooth; sauté onions in smooth mixture 2-4 minutes. Pour in seafood contents and marinade and cook until shrimp is no longer pink: add rice or lo mein and mix together. Empty onto individual dishes and top with bell pepper, pepper, and scallions

Chapter III - Soups

sssssssssssssssssssssssssssssssssssssssssssssss

21) Chinese Chicken Soup

List of Ingredients:

<u>Marinade</u>

- 1 cup chicken shredded
- 1 tbsp. organic honey
- ½ tbsp. brown sugar
- ½ tbsp. low sodium soy sauce
- 1 tsp. garlic salt
- 1 tsp. ginger powder

<u>Soup</u>

- 3 cups chicken broth
- 2 cup water
- 1 tbsp. brown sugar
- 1 egg white
- 1 cup white mushrooms cleaned and sliced
- 1 cups worth rice noodles (ramen noodles work in a pinch)
- ½ tsp. fresh or dried thyme

sssssssssssssssssssssssssssssssssssssssssssssssssss

Procedure:

In a plastic bag or air tight container mix together all ingredients for marinade and let sit in refrigerator overnight. Bring chicken broth and water to a boil, reduce heat and add remaining ingredients except egg white. Let simmer 7-9 minutes and stir so that the liquid maintains its circular motion and insert threads of egg white; turn of burner and let sit 1-2 minutes. **Serving Sizes:** 4-6

22) Peppered beef and lo mein noodle soup

List of Ingredients:

- 2 tbsp. vegetable oil
- ½ pound beef strips
- 1 grated ginger
- 2 tbsp. low sodium soy sauce
- 1 tbsp. brown sugar
- 2 bell peppers wash and seeded, cut into strips
- 1 small onion cut into strips
- ½ cup diced broccoli
- ½ cup cubed firm tofu
- 1 cup low mein noodles
- 4 cups beef broth

sssssssssssssssssssssssssssssssssssssssssssssssssssss

Procedure:

In a plastic bag or air tight container put in oil, beef strips, ginger, soy sauce, brown sugar, peppers, onion, broccoli, and tofu; keep in refrigerator 3-4 hours. Pour ingredients into large pot and brown the beef and pour in the beef broth. Let come to a boil and turn down to low. Pour in the noodles and let simmer 10 minutes.

23) Coconut Rice Soup

Inspired by the cooking of southeastern Asian, this recipe can easily become the entrée for meatless Mondays!

Serving Sizes: 4-6

List of Ingredients:

- 3 cups chicken broth or stock
- 1-2 cups water (depending on how 'brothy' tasting you like it)
- 2 cups uncooked rice
- 1 cup coconut flakes
- 1 cup snow peas
- 1 tsp. soy sauce
- 1 tsp. ginger grated or powder
- ½ tsp. red pepper flakes or sriracha sauce
- Garnish item
- Lotus pedals (optional)

ssssssssssssssssssssssssssssssssssssssssssssssssss

Procedure:

In a large pot, or Dutch oven, pour in chicken stock/broth and water and bring to a boil. Add the uncooked rice and bring pot to boil again while stirring. Once at a boil reduce heat and slowly add remaining ingredients. Let cook 40-45 minutes stirring occasionally. Top with parsley, broccoli, spinach, mushrooms, or scallions.

* Adding pre-cooked meat is ok and will not change the recipe.

**can be cooked in crockpot on high 3-4 hours

24) Not-so-traditional Wonton Soup

This soup is new version we are sure you'll find excellent, even if served over rice and your favorite veggie combos. If, you would rather make the traditional Wonton Soup just add the Wontons without the filling.

Serving Sizes: 5-7

List of Ingredients:

- 1 package wonton wrappers
- 4 cups chicken broth
- 1 package rice noodles
- 2 green onions, chopped
- ½ ginger piece
- 1 celery stalk, washed and uncut with leaves removed
- 1 chopped and seeded red pepper (jalapeno or habanero if you like hotter foods)
- 2 cloves garlic
- 8-10 shrimp, cleaned, deveined, and de-tailed

- ½ pound ground pork or ground turkey
- ½ tub button mushrooms, washed
- ½ chopped bok choy, spinach or kale
- 1 tbsp. soy sauce
- 1 tsp sesame oil (optional)

ssssssssssssssssssssssssssssssssssssssssssssssssssss

Procedure:

Place diced green onions, ginger piece, celery sticks, and red pepper into a cheesecloth or coffee filter tied at the top to prohibit the ingredients for escaping and set down inside a large pot with 4 cups of chicken broth.; let diffuse for 20 minutes. Meanwhile, in a blender or food processor blend together, shrimp, pork/turkey, mushrooms, bok choy/spinach/kale, soy sauce, sesame oil.

Set out flat multiple Wonton wrappers take 1-2 tsp of mixture and put in the middle of wrappers. Fold and set down in the broth after removing cheesecloth/ filter. Bring pot to boil and let wonton cook 4-6 minutes; before serving sprinkle with rice noodles.

25) Hot and Sour Soup

Great for colds! Very versatile soup, feel free to adjust the broth to water ratio to fit your needs, make the soup as hot as you wish by changing the peppers, and add whatever veggies you desire , and raw egg if you wish.

Serving Sizes: 4-6

List of Ingredients:

- 1 cup shredded pork, shrimp or scallops

Marinade:

- 1 tsp. soy sauce
- 2 tsp. brown sugar
- 1 tsp. vegetable oil or sesame oil

Soup List of Ingredients:

- 3 cups chicken broth or stock
- 2 cups water
- 1 cup cubed tofu (optional)
- 1 tsp. chili powder or cayenne pepper
- 1 piece of ginger minced or grated
- 3 Thyme sprigs finely chopped
- 3 Basil leaves finely chopped
- ¼ cup bean sprouts or bamboo shouts
- ¼ cup shitake mushrooms
- 1 tbsp. diced roasted red peppers (optional)
- 1 diced scallion
- 1 can cannellini beans (optional)

SSSSSSSSSSSSSSSSSSSSSSSSSSSSSSSSSSSSSSSSSSSSSSSSSS

Procedure:

Place meat or seafood along with marinade ingredients into a plastic bag or air tight container and let sit in the refrigerator 45 minutes. Meanwhile prepare soup ingredients. When ready empty the marinade ingredients into a pot (if using pork separate the meat from the marinade before cooking; raw pork can cause illness so do not cook the marinade) Cook the pork until no longer pink or running juices and, one by one, add the soup ingredients except for the scallions. Put the scallions on top of soup before serving.

26) 5 Ingredient Egg Drop Soup

An old homemade recipe; **Serving Sizes:** 4-5

List of Ingredients:

- 4 cups chicken broth
- 2 tsp. celery salt
- 1 tsp. ginger
- 1 tsp. turmeric
- 3 eggs, lightly beaten

ssssssssssssssssssssssssssssssssssssssssssssssssssss

Procedure:

Place first four ingredients into a large pot and bring to a boil over medium high heat. While waiting, beat lightly eggs. Stir the boil broth so that the water continues to move in a circular pattern and slowly introduce strands of the egg mix into the broth.

27) Broccoli Soup

A great soup to use seasonal vegetables such as butternut squash, winter squash, etc. For this soup any melon will do just remember to put them in the hot broth right before serving or else they will get mushy.

List of Ingredients:

- 3 cups chicken stock or broth, low sodium
- 1 piece of ginger, grated or minced
- 2 tsp. low sodium soy sauce
- 1 tbsp. sugar
- 1 tsp. red pepper flakes or white pepper
- Dash fennel or star anise
- 1 cucumber diced
- 1 eggplant diced
- ½ cup small broccoli pieces and trees
- 1 cup cubed melon pieces
- Cornstarch for thickening (optional)

sssssssssssssssssssssssssssssssssssssssssssssssssssss

Procedure:

Place first 6 ingredients in a pot, or Dutch oven, mix well and bring to a boil. Reduce heat and add cucumbers, eggplant, and broccoli; add the melon just before serving.

Serving Sizes: 4

28) Tofu Ma Po

List of Ingredients:

- ½ pound ground turkey or pork
- ½ cup crumbled tofu
- 2 cup honey
- 2 tbsp. brown sugar
- 1 tsp. minced ginger
- 1 tbsp. low sodium soy sauce
- 2 tsp. chili powder, cayenne pepper, paprika or ½ tsp. turmeric
- 2 tsp. sesame oil
- 10 oz. can black beans, washed and drained, (optional)
- 2-3 diced scallions for garnish

sssssssssssssssssssssssssssssssssssssssssssssssssssss

Procedure:

In plastic bag or air tight container mix together first seven ingredients and let sit in the refrigerator 2-4 hours. Heat oil in wok or skillet and empty the contents of bag/container, stir around and let cook 2-3 minutes. If using beans add them after tofu mix cooks and let warm as stirring into tofu mix. Remove and top with scallions; **Serving Sizes:** 4

29) West Lake Steak

List of Ingredients:

- ½ pound beef strips
- 1 tbsp. sugar
- 2 tbsp. low sodium soy sauce
- 1 tbsp. vegetable oil
- 1 tsp sesame oil (optional)
- ½ cup diced celery, onion, and ginger
- 3 cups chicken broth, low sodium
- 2 eggs white
- Cornstarch (for thickening, optional)

sssssssssssssssssssssssssssssssssssssssssssssssssss

Procedure:

Put the first 6 ingredients into a plastic bag or air tight container and marinade in the refrigerator overnight. Empty contents of marinade into strainer and place steak into large pot or Dutch oven and cook until steak is brown. Pour chicken broth into pot along with steak and bring to a boil, reduce heat but stir until broth maintains circular motion and stream egg whites into liquid one thread at a time. **Serving Sizes:** 4

30) Corn Soup

List of Ingredients:

- 3 cups homemade chicken stock
- 1 can creamed corn
- 1 can condensed cream of chicken soup
- 1 tbsp. mushroom pieces, washed and finely diced
- 1 tbsp. broccoli pieces or scallions
- 2 egg whites
- 1 tsp sesame oil
- 1/3 cup diced ham (optional)

sssssssssssssssssssssssssssssssssssssssssssssssssssss

Procedure:

In separate bowl beat egg lightly; set aside. In a large pot, or Dutch oven, over medium high heat bring stock, corn, cream of chicken, mushrooms, broccoli, oil and if using ham to a boil stirring well. Stir so that the soup maintains a circular motion drop strands of egg into mixture. **Serving Sizes:** 3

Chapter IV - Main Dishes

SSSSSSSSSSSSSSSSSSSSSSSSSSSSSSSSSSSSSSSSSSSSSSSSSSSSS

31) Orange Chicken

There are endless options with this chicken; it is great with rice, noodles, a variety of vegetables, and even in egg rolls!

List of Ingredients:

Marinade:

- 1 cup orange juice
- 1 tsp. orange peel
- 1 tbsp. low sodium soy sauce
- 1 tbsp. brown sugar
- 2 tsp. red pepper flakes
- 1 tsp. black pepper
- 2 tsp. minced garlic, or 3 garlic cloves (optional)
- 4 cubed boneless, skinless chicken pieces, white or dark meat

<u>Frying:</u>

- 1 egg white
- ½ cup flour
- 2 tbsp. cornstarch (more if needed)
- ½ cup water (more if too thick)
- Vegetable oil, for cooking

sssssssssssssssssssssssssssssssssssssssssssssssssssss

Procedure:

In plastic bag or sealed bowl mix all the ingredients for the marinade together and let chill overnight in the refrigerator. In another bowl mix together all the ingredients for the batter; strain the chicken and pour pieces into batter. Heat skillet or wok and oil over medium high heat and cook chicken pieces 3-5 minutes.

WARNING: eating undercooked chicken poses a major health hazard; ensure it is done before consuming. A longer cooking time will not hurt or take away from the dish.

32) General Tso Chicken

Great as a main dish or an appetizer!

Serving Sizes: 4 if served as dish with rice.

List of Ingredients:

Marinade:

- 1 recipe Kickin Hoisin Sauce
- 3 boneless, skinless chicken breasts fillets cut into cubes
- Red pepper flakes or 1 jalapeno pepper (optional)
- 1 tsp. corn starch

Sauce:

- 2 tbsp. vegetable oil
- Kickin Hoisin Sauce

Fry:

- 2 cups vegetable oil or enough for frying
- 4 eggs
- 3 cups all-purpose flour
- 2 cups cornstarch
- 1 tbsp. baking soda
- 1 tsp. baking powder

SSSSSSSSSSSSSSSSSSSSSSSSSSSSSSSSSSSSSSSSSSSSSSSSSSSSS

Procedure:

In a bowl mix together all of the ingredients for the marinade; in a plastic bag or air tight container place 1 /2 cup of the marinade along with the chicken pieces and let sit in the refrigerator 45 minutes to 1 hour.

While chicken is marinating mix together vegetable oil and the remain Hoisin Sauce and let simmer checking and stirring occasionally

After marinating, remove chicken, strain and let dry. Meanwhile beat eggs in one bowl and flour, cornstarch, baking soda and baking powder in another. Toss in the eggs and dredge through cornstarch mixture. Place a few pieces at a time into vegetable oil and cook, placing finished pieces on a paper towel.

Either serve over rice and pour the sauce over chicken or serve the chicken as appetizers with the sauce as its dipping sauce.

33) Shiitake Lo Mein

For the sake of authenticity and for easy clean up use a banana leaf instead of a plate.

Serving Sizes: 4

List of Ingredients:

- ½ tsp. onion powder
- ½ tsp. garlic powder
- 1 tsp. garlic (minced or ground)
- 1 tsp. red pepper flakes (chili or cayenne will work in a pinch)
- 2 tbsp. low sodium soy sauce
- 1 tbsp. water
- 1 tbsp. vegetable oil
- ½ pound shiitake mushroom, cleaned and de-stemmed
- ½ pound lo mein noodles
- Fennel seed or anise (optional)
- Snow peas, bok choy, water chestnuts (optional)

sssssssssssssssssssssssssssssssssssssssssssssssssssss

Procedure:

Make noodles according to package directions; meanwhile, in small bowl mix together onion and garlic powder, garlic, red pepper flakes, soy sauce, water, oil and set a aside. If using any vegetables that need to cook add them to the water in with the noodles a few minutes before straining. In a wok or skillet over med/high heat add the drained noodles; add the sauce, and the mushrooms. Stir well and cook for roughly 1 minute.

34) Tempura Chicken Lo Mein

Also great with shrimp, it can be turned into soups, salads, subs, or used as a pizza topping.

Serving Sizes: 4

List of Ingredients:

- 4 boneless, skinless chicken breasts or thighs, cubed
- 1 cup all-purpose flour
- 1 tbsp. baking soda
- 1 tsp. baking powder
- 1 tsp. celery salt
- ½ tsp. chili powder
- ¾ cup milk
- Vegetable oil, enough to fry chicken pieces
- Lo mein noodles
- Diced carrots and peas
- Cashews (optional)

sssssssssssssssssssssssssssssssssssssssssssssssssssss

Procedure:

In a large bowl mix together flour, baking soda, baking powder, chili powder, celery salt, and milk. Drop chicken into mix and place, a few at a time, in skillet or pot and fry 3-5 minutes or until golden brown. After frying place on a paper towel until all pieces are cooked. Make noodles according to package and drain. In pot combine noodles, chicken, and vegetables.

35) Baby Back Ribs in Kicked Up Hoisin Sauce

Baked baby backs are excellent with a lot of Chinese favorite but according to take out trends this is the most popular. So here is a quick, simple, healthier, and less expensive way to make it at home. Makes enough for 2 racks of ribs; however, you can do one and save the leftover sauce in an air tight container in your refrigerator

List of Ingredients:

- Kicked Up Hoisin Sauce
- 1 tsp. garlic powder
- 1 tbsp. brown sugar
- 1 tsp. chili powder or cayenne powder
- 1 tsp. ginger, fresh and minced or dried
- ½ tsp. fennel seed (optional)
- 2 tbsp. low sodium soy sauce
- 2 racks of baby back ribs

SSSSSSSSSSSSSSSSSSSSSSSSSSSSSSSSSSSSSSSSSSSSSSSSSSS

Procedure:

Depending on how m much sauce you like on your ribs you might need to double the sauce recipe.

Apply half of the sauce to the ribs and let sit in a plastic bag in the refrigerator 12-15 hours. Preheat oven to 350. Remove from plastic and place on a roasting sheet placed on top of a deep baking pan. Make sure the rack is secure and can hold some weight as your ribs will be laying on top of it. Pour approx. 2 cups water into the bottom of the pan and various herbs and spices to enhance the flavor of the ribs.

Thyme, parsley, oregano, orange or lemon peel or juice, and pineapple chunks are just a few possible additions.

Place ribs on rack and let roast for thirty-forty minutes; remove and coat with half the sauce and let cook another thirty to thirty five minutes. Remove a third time and apply the last cooking coat. Try to get front and back if possible. Cook 15-18 minutes and remove from oven; let cool for 8 minutes. Before cutting and serving if there is any remaining sauces apply it now.

36) Sweet and Sour Pork

Grilled meats and veggies add interesting depth of flavor to this recipe.

Serving Sizes: 3

List of Ingredients:

- 1 recipe sweet and sour sauce
- 1 package kielbasa sausage, cut into coin sized pieces
- 1 red pepper chopped and seeded
- 1 green pepper chopped and seeded
- 1 cup jasmine rice
- 1 ½ cup water

sssssssssssssssssssssssssssssssssssssssssssssssssssss

Procedure:

In a large pot or wok over high heat bring uncooked rice and water to a boil constantly stirring. Turn heat down to medium-low and add sausage pieces, red & green peppers, and sauce. Stir together all ingredients making sure all is coated with sauce and let simmer for 30-45 minutes stirring occasionally.

37) Quick and Tasty Egg Rolls

It has been my experience with egg rolls that the hardest part is rolling them; hopefully this recipe will help with that! And, even if they do fall apart it just adds to the fun of meals with family and/or friends.

Serving Sizes: 6-8

List of Ingredients:

- 1 package of egg roll wraps
- 1 pound lean ground beef, browned and drained
- Vegetable oil
- 1 cup Chinese cabbage
- 1/3 cup diced Bok choy
- 1/3 cup diced eggplant
- ½ tsp. ginger
- ½ tsp. chili or cayenne pepper
- 2 tbsp. low sodium soy sauce
- 1 tsp. cornstarch
- 1 tsp. rice vinegar or sesame oil (optional)

sssssssssssssssssssssssssssssssssssssssssssssssssssss

Procedure:

In a small pot cook beef until browned and strain; place on a paper towel to finish draining. Let sit for at least 5 minutes. In another bowl mix together cabbage, bok choy, eggplant, ginger, pepper, soy sauce, cornstarch, vinegar or oil if using, and ground beef. On cleaned counter top covered in parchment paper, plate, or a baking sheet lay out egg roll wrappers flat. Take ¼ -1/5 cup of mixture approx. 2 inches from the bottom corner and spread evenly lengthwise. Follow the diagram for the rest.

If the wrapper does not stick to itself, apply water or egg white to the edges via your fingertip.

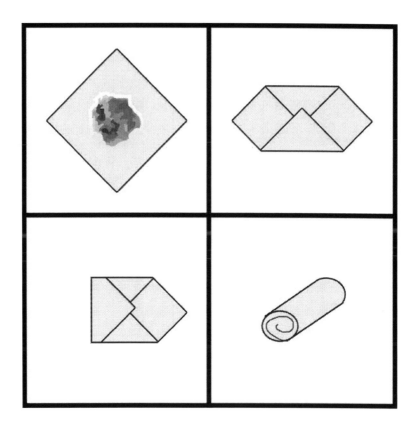

Ensure pot is free of any grease or water, it must be dry. Fill half way with vegetable oil and fry egg rolls until a golden brown. Only add a few egg rolls at a time to cook, they will not come out right if they are crowded. Also, keep an eye on the oil levels.

38) Kung Pao Shrimp

As shown in the picture this recipe is easily modified to fit all occasions and palettes. Various meats, vegetables, legumes, noodles and rice's accommodate nicely this dish.

List of Ingredients:

- 1 tbsp. vegetable oil
- 1 can pineapple and juice (optional)

Marinade:

- 1 pound medium to large shrimp
- 1 tbsp. low sodium soy sauce
- 1 tbsp. sesame oil
- 1 tsp. brown sugar
- 1 tsp. chili powder
- 1 tsp. orange peel
- ½ piece of ginger minced or grated or 2 tsp. dried ground ginger
- 2 tsp. rice wine, balsamic vinegar, or sherry

sssssssssssssssssssssssssssssssssssssssssssssssssss

Procedure:

In a plastic bag or air tight container marinade ingredients overnight in refrigerator; warm oil in wok or skillet and empty contents of marinade bag/container and let cook, while stirring around, 2-3 minutes or until shrimp is no longer pink. Remove from heat and pour in pineapple and juice, stir thoroughly together, and top with scallions. **Serving Sizes:** 3-4

39) Shiitake Lo Mein

For the sake of authenticity and for easy clean up use a banana leaf instead of a plate.

Serving Sizes: 4

List of Ingredients:

- ½ tsp. onion powder
- ½ tsp. garlic powder
- 1 tsp. garlic (minced or ground)
- 1 tsp. red pepper flakes (chili or cayenne will work in a pinch)
- 2 tbsp. low sodium soy sauce
- 1 tbsp. water
- 1 tbsp. vegetable oil
- ½ pound shiitake mushroom, cleaned and de-stemmed
- ½ pound lo mein noodles
- Fennel seed or anise (optional)
- Snow peas, bok choy, water chestnuts (optional)

sssssssssssssssssssssssssssssssssssssssssssssssssssss

Procedure:

Make noodles according to package directions; meanwhile, in small bowl mix together onion and garlic powder, garlic, red pepper flakes, soy sauce, water, oil and set a aside. If using any vegetables that need to cook add them to the water in with the noodles a few minutes before straining. In a wok or skillet over med/high heat add the drained noodles; add the sauce, and the mushrooms. Stir well and cook for roughly 1 minute.

40) Beef and Bok Choy

A new version of the well-worn beef and broccoli,

Serving Sizes: 4

List of Ingredients:

- 1 tbsp. vegetable oil
- 1 pound beef strips
- 1 cup jasmine rice
- 1 cup water
- 1 tbsp. pineapple juice
- 2 tsp. low sodium soy sauce
- 1 tsp. beef bullion
- 1 tbsp. sesame oil
- 1 tbsp. brown sugar
- ½ ginger, grated
- 3 tsp. cornstarch
- 1 cup diced bok choy
- 1 cup of diced shitake mushrooms
- 1 tbsp. pinenuts or walnuts

sssssssssssssssssssssssssssssssssssssssssssssssssssss

Procedure:

Place all ingredients into a crockpot and stir well; cook on low for 90 minutes. After 90 minutes add to the beef mix bok choy, mushrooms, and legumes stir, and let cook on low another 10 minutes.

This recipe is so simple it welcomes substitutions and additions, here are a few possibilities:

- Spinach or kale for the bok choy
- Peppers
- Broccoli and cauliflower
- Baby corn
- Rice noodles
- Tofu

Add more beef bouillon, leave out the rice and make a soup

Leave out the rice and serve over lo mein noodles

Shrimp or sausage for the beef

41) Shrimp Lo Mein

For an extra kick double up on the red pepper flakes. Get creative and try this recipe with a variety of vegetables such as: broccoli, baby corn, snow peas, and bok choy!

Serving Sizes: 3-5

List of Ingredients:

- ½ pound lo mein noodles
- 1 tbsp. vegetable oil
- 3 tsp. onion powder
- 3 tsp. garlic powder
- 1 tsp. red pepper flakes
- 1 tsp. ginger, minced if fresh
- 1 tbsp. low sodium soy sauce
- 1 stalk of celery finely diced
- ¼ cup of eggplant finely diced
- 1/3 cup tofu diced or cubed
- 1 tsp. sesame oil
- 1 ½ tbsp. cornstarch
- 1 tbsp. water
- 1 pound medium to large shrimp

SS

Procedure:

Place into a plastic bag or covered bowl to marinade: vegetable oil, onion and garlic powders, red pepper flakes, ginger, soy sauce, and shrimp. Let sit 4 hours to overnight and before cooking shrimp prepare the noodles al dente according to directions on the package. Empty contents of the bag into a wok or skillet over medium high heat and sauté for 30-45 seconds then add celery, eggplant, tofu, oil, cornstarch, water and lo mein noodles. Cook until all is heated through and shrimp is no longer pink.

42) Fried Rice

The perfect accommodation too many a dish and stir-fry presented here with new flavors! For something different try fried rice with chicken bouillon instead of beef and either eliminate or substitute honey or pineapple juice for the brown sugar; best when paired with orange chicken or sweet and sour pork!

Serving Sizes: 2-3

List of Ingredients:

- 1 cup jasmine
- 1 cup water
- Pineapple juice (drained juice from can into rice)
- 2 tsp. beef bullion
- 1 tbsp. brown sugar
- ½ celery salt or flakes
- 1/3 tsp. garlic salt
- ½ ginger, minced
- ½ tsp. cayenne or chili powder
- 1/3 cup diced carrot
- ½ cup crushed pineapple

- ½ cup peas or snow peas

ssssssssssssssssssssssssssssssssssssssssssssssssssss

Procedure:

In large pot, or Dutch oven, over high heat combine all ingredients except carrots, pineapple, and peas; stir well and bring to a boil Turn heat down to low and add vegetables; let simmer 45 minutes. Checking every 7-9 minutes and stirring.

43) Spiced Tofu

Traditionally an appetizer, this recipe pairs it with mushrooms and rice to bring you a tasty meal!

Serving Sizes: 2

List of Ingredients:

- ½ block extra firm tofu cut into 1 x 1 cubes, or 2 cup pre-cubed extra firm tofu
- ¾ cup cornstarch
- 3 tsp. black pepper
- 3 tsp. ginger
- 1 cup jasmine rice
- 1 ½ cup water
- 1 tbsp. vegetable oil
- ½ tub button mushrooms, cleaned
- 1 finely diced bok choy
- 1 cup baby corn
- ¼ cup scallions
- 2 tbsp. low sodium soy sauce
- 1 tbsp. grated ginger
- 1 tsp. brown sugar

SSS

Procedure:

Prepare rice and water in steamer or on stovetop. In a skillet or wok over medium high heat sauté mushrooms, bok choy, baby corn, and scallions in vegetable oil; set aside when cooked through roughly 2 minutes. In a bowl mix together soy sauce, ginger, and brown sugar; mix well and set aside. Pat tofu dry and mix together tofu, cornstarch, black pepper, and ginger making sure all pieces are covered. Fill skillet or wok with vegetable oil and fry tofu pieces, a few at a time, until golden brown. Remove tofu and place on a paper towel. Add tofu and vegetables to the rice and pour the soy sauce mixture over and mix together

Chapter V - Sauces

ssssssssssssssssssssssssssssssssssssssssssssssssss

44) Honey Teriyaki for Grilling

This sauce is good for all grilling meats but really goes great with chicken!

List of Ingredients:

- 2 cup orange juice
- ½ cup organic honey
- ¼ cup brown sugar
- 2 tsp. minced or grated fresh ginger or dried and ground
- 1 tsp. chili powder or red pepper flakes
- 1 finely diced green onion or 1 tsp. finely diced basil
- 1 1/3 cup low sodium soy sauce
- 1 tbsp. cornstarch

sssssssssssssssssssssssssssssssssssssssssssssssssssssss

Procedure:

Mix ingredients together and stir well; let chili in refrigerator 45 minutes. Put on meats 15 minutes before finished.

45) Easy Homemade Sweet and Sour

This is a homemade sauce, so it tastes a bit different from that found in commercial establishments. However, it is a great sauce for beef, pork, shrimp, veggies, stir-fry's and egg rolls!

Serving Sizes: approximately ¾ - 1 cup.

List of Ingredients:

- ½ cup rice vinegar
- 5 tbsp. brown sugar
- 1 1/3-½ ketchup
- 1 1/3-½ low sodium soy sauce
- 3 tsp. cornstarch diluted into 5 tsp. of water

sssssssssssssssssssssssssssssssssssssssssssssssssssss

Procedure:

Mix all ingredients together and let sit for at least 5 minutes sauce will thicken. If you desire thicker sauce add more cornstarch. Can be made in advance if kept in an air tight container; however, stir well before adding it to any dish.

As with any recipe some merely tolerate it and others can't even do that. Here are some suggestions for substitutions:

- Apple cider vinegar or white vinegar for the rice vinegar
- Chili powder for the ketchup
- Diced green pepper or jalapeno
- 1 cup Crushed pineapple and the juice

46) Take 5 Peanut Sauce

A delicious peanut sauce in just five simple ingredients! Yields approx. ¾- 1 cup; store in refrigerator 3-5 days in an air tight container.

List of Ingredients:

- 3 tbsp. soy sauce
- ½ - ¾ cup peanut butter
- 2 tbsp. hot water
- 3 tbsp. rice vinegar
- 1 tsp red pepper flakes

sssssssssssssssssssssssssssssssssssssssssssssssssssss

Procedure:

Mix ingredients together and let chill in refrigerator a minimum of 3 hours.

47) 1 Hour BBQ Sauce

Takes 5 minutes to put together and is great as a sauce for meats or as a marinate; also works as a dipping sauce. If kept in an air tight container this sauce stay good 5-7 days.

Serving Sizes: approximately 1- 1 ½ cups

List of Ingredients:

- 6 tsp. oyster sauce
- ¼ cup hoisin sauce
- 2 tsp. sesame oil
- 1 tbsp. rice wine
- 1 tbsp. low sodium soy sauce
- 1 tsp. ginger or ½ tsp. turmeric (for a hotter sauce add more turmeric 1 tsp at a time)

sssssssssssssssssssssssssssssssssssssssssssssssssss

Procedure:

Place in a small bowl and mix together.

48) 300 Second Sauce

A delicious sauce for potstickers, dumpling, and egg rolls! 1 recipe yields ½ cup; will keep 4 days in air tight container in refrigerator.

List of Ingredients:

- 2 tbsp. rice vinegar
- 8 tbsp. soy sauce
- 2 tsp. red pepper flakes
- 2 tsp. celery salt
- ½ tsp. orange peel
- 1 tsp. sugar
- 1 tsp. ginger (optional)

sssssssssssssssssssssssssssssssssssssssssssssssssssss

Procedure:

In bowl mix together and let sit at least thirty minutes before serving.

49) Ginger Thyme Oil

This sauce is easily amendable as ginger can be paired with lots of vegetables to better accommodate any dish. This sauce is best served with seafood's such as scallops or shrimp but also pairs well with various types of fish.

Serving Sizes: approx. 1 cup

List of Ingredients:

- ¼ - 1/3 cup thyme
- 2-3 inch piece of ginger, washed and peeled, grated or minced
- ¼ - 1/3 cup peanut oil
- 1 diced stalk of bok choy (optional)
- ½ cup cubed firm tofu (optional)

sssssssssssssssssssssssssssssssssssssssssssssssss

Procedure:

Over medium/ high heat let the peanut oil sit for 4-6 minutes (approx. 300 degrees). Meanwhile mix together thyme and ginger; add to oil when sufficiently hot. Mix together, mixture might sizzle, let sit 3-6 seconds and remove.

Some like their sauce spicy so here are some suggestions for additions:

- Red pepper flakes
- Diced green peppers
- Cumin
- Turmeric
- Chili or cayenne powder

50) Kicked Up Hoisin Sauce

Great for stir-fry's and a dipping sauce, one recipe will make between 1/3 and ¾ cup.

This sauce is best if used immediately but will keep in the refrigerator 3-4 days if kept in an air tight container.

List of Ingredients:

- 1 tsp. garlic powder
- 1 tbsp. brown sugar
- 1 tsp. chili powder or cayenne powder
- 1 tsp. ginger, fresh and minced or dried
- ½ tsp. fennel seed (optional)
- 2 tbsp. low sodium soy sauce

ssssssssssssssssssssssssssssssssssssssssssssssssssssssss

Procedure:

Mix sauce ingredients together and let heat in wok over high heat; once heated pour in stir-fry ingredients and cook over medium heat. If using as a dipping sauce just pour mix ingredients into pot and let simmer 20-30 minutes or until becomes fragrant and smooth.

51) Oriental Vinaigrette

Some use Chinese 5 spice in this vinaigrette and others use All-spice instead of the ginger, pepper, and parsley. Either way this is a great dressing for salads and 1 batch provides enough for ½ - ¾ cups. You can make this 3-5 day in advance if kept in an air tight container in the refrigerator.

List of Ingredients:

- ¾ cup olive oil
- 3 tsp. low sodium soy sauce
- 2 ½ tsp. sugar
- 1/3 cup rice vinegar
- 2 tsp. pineapple juice
- 1 tsp. ginger (fresh or dried)
- 1 tsp. black pepper
- 1 tsp. of parsley (cilantro or fennel can be substituted)

sssssssssssssssssssssssssssssssssssssssssssssssssssss

Procedure:

Place in a small bowl and mix together.

52) Tangy Teriyaki Sauce

A simple sauce that takes teriyaki to a whole other level! Great for fish; make 3-4 days in advance and keep in the refrigerator in an air tight container.

Serving Sizes: approx. 1 - 1 ¼ cup

List of Ingredients:

- 2 tbsp. soy sauce
- 1 ½ tsp. rice vinegar
- 2 tbsp. sunflower or coconut oil
- 1/3 grated or minced fresh ginger or 2 tsp. dried ginger
- 1 tsp. celery salt or flakes
- 1/3 sugar or brown sugar
- ½ tsp. red pepper flakes

sssssssssssssssssssssssssssssssssssssssssssssssssssss

Procedure:

In a small bowl mix all ingredients together.

53) T.A.G Sauce

A marinade that is great with tofu! Will keep in the refrigerator 3-5 days if kept in an air tight container;

Serving Sizes: approx. 1-2 cups

List of Ingredients:

- 2 tsp. garlic powder
- 5 cherry tomatoes diced
- 2-inch piece of ginger grated or minced, 1 tbsp. dried ginger
- 1 tsp. sesame oil
- 3 tbsp. low sodium soy sauce
- 1 tbsp. organic honey or pineapple juice

sssssssssssssssssssssssssssssssssssssssssssssssssssss

Procedure:

In a bowl mix all ingredient together.

About the Author

Allie Allen developed her passion for the culinary arts at the tender age of five when she would help her mother cook for their large family of 8. Even back then, her family knew this would be more than a hobby for the young Allie and when she graduated from high school, she applied to cooking school in London. It had always been a dream of the young chef to study with some of Europe's best and she made it happen by attending the Chef Academy of London.

After graduation, Allie decided to bring her skills back to North America and open up her own restaurant. After 10 successful years as head chef and owner, she decided to sell her business and pursue other career avenues. This monumental decision led Allie to her true calling, teaching. She also started to write e-books for her students to study at home for practice. She is now the proud author of several e-books and gives private and semi-private cooking lessons to a range of students at all levels of experience.

Stay tuned for more from this dynamic chef and teacher when she releases more informative e-books on cooking and baking in the near future. Her work is infused with stores and anecdotes you will love!

Author's Afterthoughts

I can't tell you how grateful I am that you decided to read my book. My most heartfelt thanks that you took time out of your life to choose my work and I hope you find benefit within these pages.

There are so many books available today that offer similar content so that makes it even more humbling that you decided to buying mine.

Tell me what you thought! I am eager to hear your opinion and ideas on what you read as are others who are looking for a good book to buy. Leave a review on Amazon.com so others can benefit from your wisdom!

With much thanks,

Allie Allen

Printed in Great Britain
by Amazon

71009200R00066